UPSIDE-DOWN LIVING

parenting

[The *Upside-Down Living* series emphasizes living out one's Christian faith through the lens of Jesus, by following values that seem so countercultural they appear to be upside down.]

Katherine & Peter Goerzen

Harrisonburg, Virginia

**Upside-Down Living
Parenting**

© 2018 by Herald Press, Harrisonburg, Virginia 22803. 800-245-7894.
   All rights reserved.
International Standard Book Number: 978-1-5138-0404-0
Printed in United States of America
Design by Merrill Miller
Cover photo by Nadezhda1906/iStockphoto/Thinkstock

All rights reserved. This publication may not be reproduced, stored in a retrieval system, or transmitted in whole or in part, in any form, by any means, electronic, mechanical, photocopying, recording or otherwise without prior permission of the copyright owners.

Unless otherwise noted, Scripture text is quoted, with permission, from the New Revised Standard Version, © 1989, Division of Christian Education of the National Council of Churches of Christ in the United States of America.

22 21 20 19 18   10 9 8 7 6 5 4 3 2 1

TWINSTERPHOTO/ISTOCKPHOTO/THINKSTOCK

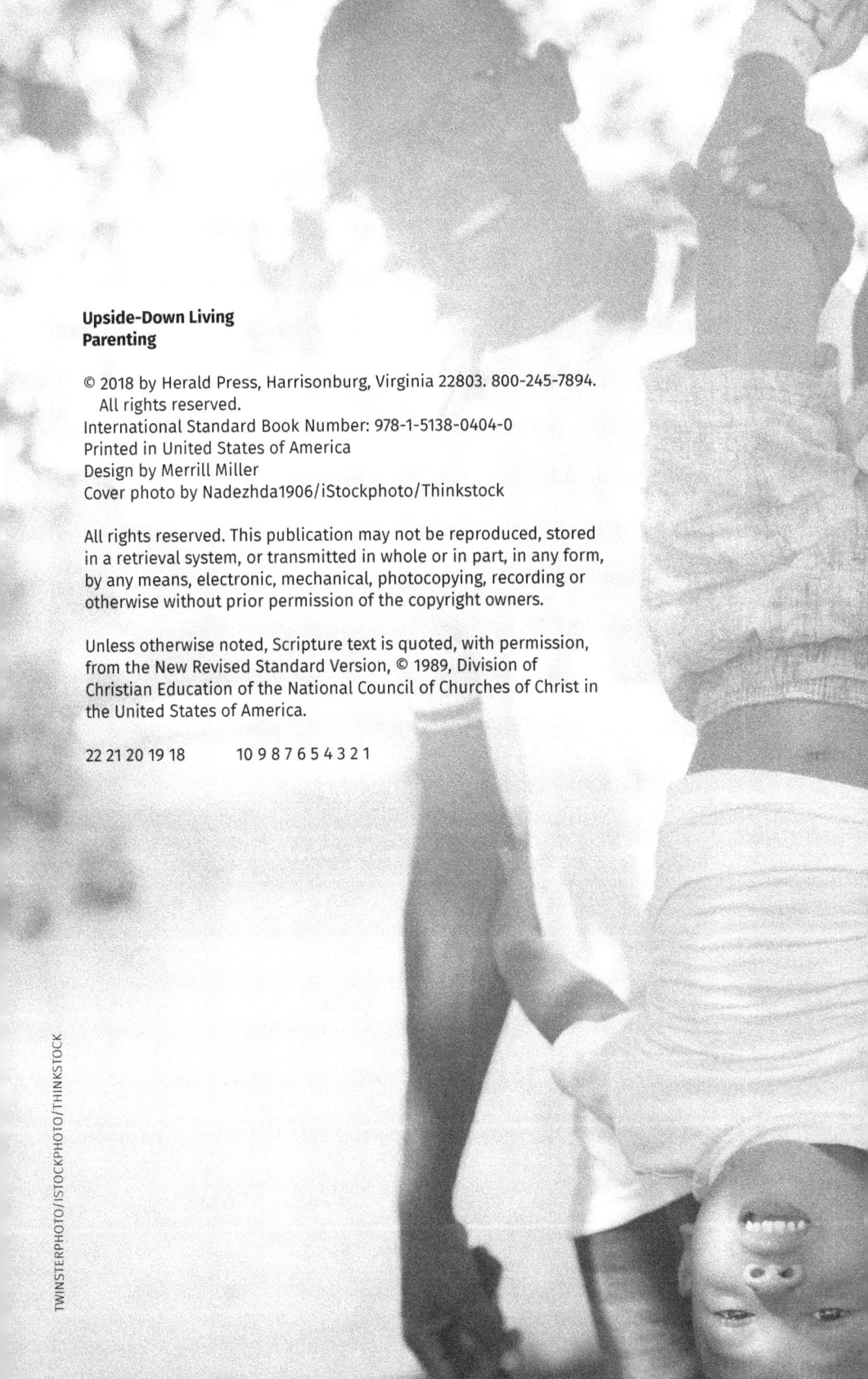

[Contents]

Introduction:
Meager Crumbs and Miraculous Blessings 5

1. **What These Stones Mean:**
The Stories Our Lives Tell 9

2. **Wonderfully Made:**
The Messages We Communicate about Bodies 15

3. **Do unto Others:**
Loving Our Neighbors—and Enemies—as Ourselves 21

4. **First Shall Be Last:**
Winning the "Jesus Way". 27

5. **Where Our Heart Is:**
How We Consume in the Upside-Down Kingdom 33

6. **In the World but Not of It:**
Engaging Culture with Our Kids 39

About the Writers 45

INTRODUCTION:
[Meager Crumbs and Miraculous Blessings]

John 6:1-14

Parenting is hard, holy work. Although we wouldn't consider ourselves experts by any means (who would?), we have done our best to embody God's upside-down way of living and to carry out the practices we've written about in this book. Sometimes we're able to do these well. Often we fall short.

Parenting is hard, holy work, even at the best of times. It's all the more difficult to embody God's patience and steadfast love when we're overwhelmed by the myriad anxieties we're carrying. It's difficult to engage with our children in meaningful ways when we're exhausted and still have many things to check off our to-do lists.

Parenting is hard, holy work. It's so easy to feel we're not doing enough, that we're not able to be a good enough example, that what we *can* offer our kids won't be enough to make a difference.

One of the few stories that makes an appearance in all four gospels is the story of Jesus feeding the crowd of more than five thousand. It was late, and Jesus knew that the crowd would be hungry. So he told his disciples to give the people something to eat. All they were able to come up with were five small loaves and two smelly fish. The disciples could not possibly imagine how these mere crumbs would be enough to feed such a large crowd. Yet Jesus took what they had, broke and blessed their gifts, and multiplied them abundantly for the sake of all who had gathered.

Some days we might feel that all we can offer our children are meager crumbs. Some days the tasks ahead of us seem impossible. Some days what we have given on behalf of our children just doesn't seem to be enough.

> [**Even our brokenness** can be blessed by God.]

Yet God takes even our meager crumbs and blesses them; even our brokenness can be blessed by God. God meets us where we are, reminding us that nothing is impossible for God. God works through us, using the gifts that we offer, no matter how small, to work miracles for the sake of the kingdom.

The upside-down values and practices that we outline in this study are by no means an exhaustive list of gifts we as parents can offer to shape our children's lives. In parenting our own two young children and in our pastoral work with high schoolers and college-age young adults (in congregations and on a college campus), we know that the topics mentioned in this study reflect where we are at this time and the kingdom values we have most felt called to instill in our children and youth. Yet parents and others who work with children and youth could add many other topics related to upside-down living. We would encourage you to prayerfully seek ways you can instill the values of God's kingdom in your children when it comes to other issues and cultural narratives.

At the end of each session are some discussion questions. You are welcome to reflect on the questions by reading and processing these by yourself, with a few friends, or with a small group or faith formation class. You can speak to these questions out loud or spend time writing reflections in a journal. You could even create "word art" by writing out a suggested passage of Scripture or drawing shapes and images that come to mind in response to the passage or discussion questions.

We hope that this study will remind you of the ways that God is already miraculously blessing the gifts you offer on behalf of your children. We pray it helps you envision new ways to practice and instill upside-down living in your family.

Blessings as you continue the hard and holy work of parenting.

—Katherine and Peter Goerzen

1 WHAT THESE STONES MEAN: The Stories Our Lives Tell

Joshua 4:1-7

Our son loves to tell stories. It is one of the ways that he makes sense of the world around him—drawing into his stories the things he sees, the people he loves, or even plots of stories that we have told him. As an active four-year-old, he rarely sits still. But he will (almost) always sit and listen when we pull out books, or when we begin telling stories from his past or family stories that have been passed down to us.

There is a power in storytelling that moves us beyond simply conveying facts and ideas. Stories draw us in. They build on our curiosity and creativity. They can stir our hearts toward empathy and compassion. Stories have the capacity to shape us, to spark our imaginations, and inspire us to hope. Jesus knew this well and was famous for telling stories and parables to awaken the imagination.

As parents, we deeply hope to instill faith in our children. We trust that God's Spirit is already present and at work in our children's hearts and minds. We can point to the ways that God is moving within our lives, within our children, and within the world. Instilling faith in our children means helping them to see themselves as part of what God is already doing in the world.

> [**The stories around us do a very good job of capturing our attention and luring us in.**]

It's also important to be aware of the many stories that are shaping us. Our values and practices are shaped by the stories we inhabit and internalize. The stories around us do a very good job of capturing our attention and luring us in. We may not even be aware of all the ways that cultural narratives are conforming us and our children to the patterns of this world.

As people committed to God's kingdom, we want to be shaped by God's story. This story includes the ways that God is revealed through Scripture, through the person of Jesus and the lives of people who follow him, and through the work of God's Spirit in the created world. Our children are waiting for us to tell the stories of God's movement in the world. These stories invite us to be active participants in God's good news.

The first thing that God's people did after they crossed over into the land of promise was build a monument to remember what God had done. Joshua 4 tells us that 12 people were asked to pick up stones from the dry riverbed and place them one on top of the other. These stones were meant to be a sign. They

were designed to evoke curiosity in their children, to prompt
them to ask, "What do those stones mean to you?" (Joshua 4:6).

The stones were erected to encourage storytelling. The answer to
their children's question lay not in clever slogans, but in recounting the story of how God has been moving in the life of God's
people. To answer their children's question was to draw them into
the story of God's steadfast love throughout history. The stones
were an ever-present reminder and sign pointing to what God
has done and continues to do.

As parents, we can be "living stones" that point our
children toward God. Our lives should tell a story that is different
from the narratives of the world. We are called to live as people
who are a part of God's story. Our habits, choices, and words can
evoke our children's curiosity and prompt them to ask, "What
does that mean? Why are you doing that?"

> [It's often when we are driving together, or when we're outside, or as we're putting our children to bed that we find space for these holy conversations.]

In parenting our own young children, and in our ministry with
youth, we have noticed that certain times and places lend themselves to these holy conversations. It's often when we are driving
together, or when we're outside, or as we're putting our children
to bed that we find space for these holy conversations.

Our children often ask why we read them Bible stories rather
than a different storybook before bed. We respond by saying that
these stories are special because they tell us about who God is and
how people experience God. We remind them that these stories

are very old, and that people have been telling them for many, many years. And when we read Bible stories with our children, we tend to read stories from the Gospels, so that they will be intimately familiar with the stories of Jesus. We want them to know him and his teachings, as well as to imagine how they can live the way he lived and experience his care and love.

The more our children internalize stories from Scripture and from us as their parents, the more they will be formed in their values, their passions, and their faith. The stones were given to the Hebrew people so that they would remember whose story they had been called to join. The stones were an ever-present sign pointing to God's activity and presence among them.

As "living stones," parents can meet children in the moments of their curiosity, equipping them with eyes to see and ears to hear the ways that God is moving in our world. We can help evoke within our children a sense of creativity and imagination, building upon the foundation that God has already laid. We can continually invite them back into God's story.

Talk about it

- ▶ Immerse yourself in the story of Joshua 4:1-7. Read through the story two or three times, preferably out loud. Notice the words or phrases that stand out to you. What strikes you? What questions do you have? How might God be speaking to you through this story? How is God calling you to respond?

- ▶ What questions have your children been asking recently?

- ▶ What stories, songs, and Scripture passages have been meaningful to you and have influenced your perception of God?

Who are some of the faithful people—the "living stones"—
who have influenced your faith?

▶ Our faith and our values are shaped by the stories that we inhabit. What are the stories we are telling our children through our words, our deeds, and our example? What are the faithful values we want our lives to nurture within our children?

▶ What are the teachable moments or spaces in which we can inspire our children's imaginations? How can we help point them to see the ways that God is already working through their lives?

▶ We are told in Joshua 4 that the Hebrew people erected a monument to remind them of what God had done and what God would continue to do. What are ways you can mark how God is working within your family? How can you remind yourself and your family of whose you are and whose story you're called to join?

Suggestions for further reading

▶ *Beyond Me: Grounding Youth Ministry in God's Story*, by Wendell J. Loewen (Faith & Life Resources, 2008)
▶ *Fledge: Launching Your Kids without Losing Your Mind*, by Brenda L. Yoder (Herald Press, 2018)
▶ *God's Story, Our Story: Exploring Christian Faith and Life*, 2nd edition, by Michele Hershberger (Herald Press, 2013)
▶ *Growing Together: Understanding and Nurturing Your Child's Faith Journey*, by Anne Neufeld Rupp (Faith & Life Press, 1996)
▶ *Ordinary Miracles: Awakening to the Holy Work of Parenting*, by Rachel S. Gerber (Herald Press, 2014)

- *Seek Peace and Pursue It: Women, Faith, and Family Care,* by Elizabeth Soto Albrecht (Faith & Life Resources, 2010)
- *Shaped by the Story: Helping Students Encounter God in a New Way,* by Michael Novelli (Zondervan, 2008)
- *Shine On: A Story Bible* (Herald Press, 2014)
- *Youth Ministry at a Crossroads: Tending to the Faith Formation of Mennonite Youth,* edited by Andy Brubacher Kaethler and Bob Yoder (Herald Press, 2011)

2 WONDERFULLY MADE:
The Messages We Communicate about Bodies

Genesis 1:26-31

As people connected to God's story, we believe that we are created good and are loved by God. Yet it is difficult to truly take this to heart, as we constantly hear the opposite. Many of the messages that we receive about our bodies—from the media, from peers, or even from family—can convince us that our bodies do not look as they should. The two of us have been studying and reading and preaching about being created in God's good image for more than ten years. And yet it is still so easy for us to believe the story the media and our culture tell us about our bodies: that we're not good enough, not beautiful enough, not worthy enough.

Having children has forced us to think intentionally about this. We are careful not to complain about our bodies while around our children. These are not the stories that we want to shape their perceptions about their own self-worth. But what if our children could come to know the truth of our bodies: that we bear God's image, and are very good?

When asked about the greatest commandment, Jesus responded: "'You shall love the Lord your God with all your heart, and with all your soul, and with all your mind, and with all your strength.' The second is this, 'You shall love your neighbor as yourself'" (Mark 12:30-31). The first session of this study focused on loving God. These next two will focus on loving our neighbor as we love ourselves.

Sometimes Christians emphasize loving our neighbors without simultaneously emphasizing loving ourselves. Yet love for neighbor and love for self go hand in hand. Given the ways that the world is constantly telling us that we aren't good enough, we need to remind our children that God's own image dwells within them. They are created "very good"; they are unconditionally and deeply loved.

> **Given the ways that the world is constantly telling us that we aren't good enough, we need to remind our children that God's own image dwells within them.**

We've tried to instill this in our children from the beginning. We hope that they will internalize this message while they are young, as we know that negative messages about their bodies will only intensify as they get to middle school and high school. Therefore we frequently tell them that their bodies are very good, that their bodies are strong, and that they have something of God within them. Instead of focusing on their looks, as advertisements and other media tend to do, we point out all the amazing things their bodies can do: run, dance, see, hear, sense, touch, create, comprehend, hold the hands of those we love.

In the beginning of God's story, in Genesis, we are told that God created all humankind in God's own image. Then God proclaimed us to be "very good," a proclamation echoed in Psalm 139, which reminds us that we are fearfully and wonderfully made by God's own hand.

> [There is something of God in both our daughters and our sons.]

Genesis 1 proclaims that God's very image dwells within all humankind. There is something of God in both our daughters and our sons. As all people are created in God's image, it stands to reason that God has characteristics that are both wonderfully masculine and wonderfully feminine. When we are mindful of the language, imagery, and stories we use to talk about God with our children, they can see God's image within themselves and other people.

No matter what the airbrushed images tell us, no one body type can fully capture the beauty of God's image. Regardless of how we look—whether we are dark or light, tall or short, male or female, old or young, or somewhere in between—the entire spectrum of human bodies speaks to the goodness and beauty of God's image reflected within humanity.

The more we can tell our children that God's good image dwells within all people—including those who look different, or think differently, or act differently—the more they internalize a story that is different from the stories of the world around us.

Our bodies are created very good, yet our worth extends beyond our bodies. We are so deeply loved by our Creator that God took on human flesh and came to dwell among us. God was even willing to die for our sake. There is nothing—"neither death, nor life, nor angels, nor rulers, nor things present, nor things to come, nor powers, nor height, nor depth, nor anything else in all creation"—that can separate us from the love of God in Christ Jesus (see Romans 8:38-39).

> No matter what they look like, no matter what choices they make, no matter who they are, we love them.

As parents, we can begin to fathom how deeply God loves us when we reflect on our love for our own children. No matter what they look like, no matter what choices they make, no matter who they are, we love them. How much more deeply does God love them. How much more deeply does God love us all!

No matter what stories that are told around us, God's story proclaims that we are worthy, we are beautiful, and we are loved deeply by our Creator, who has made us and who reminds us that we are "very good."

2. **WONDERFULLY MADE:** THE MESSAGES WE COMMUNICATE ABOUT BODIES

Talk about it

- ▶ Immerse yourself in both Genesis 1:26-31 and Psalm 139:1-18 (in particular, verses 13-16). Read through these passages two or three times, preferably out loud. Notice the words or phrases that stand out to you. What strikes you? What questions do these passages raise? What do you hear God saying about you? Your body? Your children?

- ▶ What do you think it means to be created in God's image? How can we proclaim God's story to our children in a way that begins to diminish the influence of media and advertisements that sell us short?

- ▶ Reflect on some of the aspects of your body that you celebrate (such as what your body can do, how you look, who you are, and so on). What are some of the things you would like God's help to be able to affirm about your body? What do you need to let go of to see yourself as "very good"?

- ▶ What kind of stories about the human body in general, or your body in particular, did you hear as you were growing up? How did these stories inform your own sense of self-worth? How did these stories inform your perception of other people?

- ▶ What kinds stories are your children being exposed to most often? What are they hearing or saying about the human body in general—including the human body's beautiful variety of shapes, sizes, and colors—or their own bodies in particular? In what ways are you already reminding your children of their deep worth? How can you continue to instill in them a sense of self-worth as beloved children of God? How can our lives model the deep value of every person created in God's good image, regardless of who they are, how they look, or the choices they make?

Suggestions for further reading

- *Nurturing Healthy Sexuality at Home: A Guide for Parents*, by Rachel Nafziger Hartzler (Faith & Life Resources, 2010)
- *Peaceful at Heart: Embracing Healthy Masculinity*, edited by Steve Thomas and Don Neufeld (Wipf and Stock, 2018)
- *Seven Things Children Need*, 3rd edition, by John M. Drescher (Herald Press, 2012)
- *Sex + Faith: Talking with Your Child from Birth to Adolescence*, by Kate Ott (Westminster John Knox Press, 2013)
- *Sexuality: God's Gift*, 2nd edition, edited by Anne Krabill Hershberger (Herald Press, 2010)
- *Under Construction: Reframing Men's Spirituality*, by Gareth Brandt (Herald Press, 2009)
- *Wonderfully Made*, Abundant Faith: Women's Bible Study Series (Herald Press, 2016)
- *Worthy: Finding Yourself in a World Expecting Someone Else*, by Melanie Springer Mock (Herald Press, 2018)

3 DO UNTO OTHERS: Loving Our Neighbors —and Enemies— as Ourselves

Luke 6:27-36

One day when I (Katherine) was walking home with our daughter after school, she told me, "Mom, I was praying on the playground today."

I was intrigued. "Oh really?" I asked.

"Yes. One of the boys in my class was saying mean things to me. I was praying that I could still be kind to him, even when he had been mean to me."

Children have an amazing ability to reveal Christ to us. Sometimes they remind us that being connected to God's story means loving our neighbors as ourselves. This can be an easy and joy-giving commandment when we're around people who are kind to us.

But loving our neighbors who may be very different than us takes practice. And loving our neighbors who are cruel to us or who have hurt those we love? Well, this is one part of God's story that bears repeating precisely because it is so difficult to do. And yet it is at the heart of God's good news to the world.

Part of our task as parents is to help our children see beyond the stories of "us versus them" and to point them to God's way of compassionate and costly love. As people committed to Jesus' way of peace, we frequently tell stories of peacemakers or point out situations in books or movies in which violence didn't

> **[We frequently tell stories of peacemakers or point out situations in books or movies in which violence didn't accomplish the desired outcome.]**

accomplish the desired outcome. We tell our children these stories over and over, because the cultural narrative that violence and revenge are the most effective ways to solve conflict is so prevalent. Sometimes referred to as the myth of redemptive violence, this narrative is widespread even in books and movies marketed to young children.

3. DO UNTO OTHERS: LOVING OUR NEIGHBORS—AND ENEMIES—AS OURSELVES

As our children tell us stories of hurtful words or actions from other children, we try to help them identify their feelings about what happened. We want them to learn to pay attention to feelings, which tell us when something is not right and help us identify what we need. But we also try to help them understand that when people make mean choices, they are likely hurting inside, and we help our children pray for their enemies.

> Love for others, even for enemies, is at the heart of who God is.

We are called to choose Jesus' way of love on a daily basis. We try to model and nurture actions that reflect God's deep love for all people. We are to be compassionate as God is compassionate. Love for others, even for enemies, is at the heart of who God is.

In his Sermon on the Plain, in Luke 7, Jesus exhorts the crowds to do good even to those who hate them. He follows this by telling them how to respond: by offering the other cheek when someone slaps them. To first-century ears, this gesture would have meant "You are treating me as inferior, but I deserve to be treated with respect."

Jesus wasn't calling his followers to be doormats. He was giving them a creative and compassionate way to respond to violence and hatred, a way that stopped the cycle of violence rather than perpetuated it.

This is a part of God's story that the world just doesn't seem to understand. Instead, the stories around us tell how satisfying it is to get revenge. They tell us to fear or exclude those who are from different backgrounds. These stories proclaim that compassion and nonviolence may be effective in the small things of life but not when the *real* problems arise.

Jesus' life, teaching, death, and resurrection **proclaim a much different story.**

We're called to do good to those who mistreat us, not only because statistically this is shown to be more effective but because this is at the heart of God's good news.

This, perhaps, is one of the most difficult parts of God's story to embody. It's second nature to love those who love us. But loving those who mistreat us? Although not nearly as easy, it is possible to do by nurturing a life of prayer, compassion, and creativity within ourselves and our children.

Studies have shown that children whose imaginations are limited are far more prone to violence, whereas children with fertile imaginations are more likely to reach a mutually beneficial solution when difficult situations arise. As parents, we can nurture creativity and imagination in our children. We can help them to think about different ways to respond in difficult situations, such as by offering words of kindness or a creative solution that respects the needs and feelings of all involved. Nurturing creativity includes teaching our children to be empathetic: seeing the situation from another's point of view, or pondering together why a child might be making hurtful choices. Violent behavior in children often stems from something else, such as witnessing violence at home or experiencing pain themselves.

We love our neighbors as ourselves and seek to respond creatively when conflict arises not because we're "bleeding hearts" or weak on justice. Rather, we have chosen to embody the story of the One who redefined what it means to call someone "neighbor"

(Luke 10:25-37). We follow the One whose image dwells within "the least of these" (Matthew 25:31-40). We proclaim the gospel of the One who forgave with his dying breath those who were crucifying him (Luke 23:34). This is the story to which we've given our lives and that we long to instill in our children.

Talk about it

- ▶ Immerse yourself in Jesus' teaching from Luke 6:27-36. Read through this passage two or three times, preferably out loud. Notice the words or phrases that stand out to you. What strikes you? What questions does this passage raise? Are there specific people or situations that come to mind as you read it? How might God be calling you to respond?

- ▶ Immerse yourself in the story of Abigail from 1 Samuel 25:2-35. What stands out to you about this story? What questions does it raise? How might this story creatively inspire other solutions when confronted with difficult situations?

- ▶ When have you or your family members embodied the way of love for others? What happened as a result of this compassion?

- ▶ When have you watched your children choose God's way of love? How did you respond? How did your children respond? How might you mark these moments?

- ▶ What are practices that your family is already engaged in that nurture creativity and compassion within your children? (These might include things like games, service projects, movies, family meetings, or conversations about current events.) What practices could you add?

Suggestions for further reading

- *How to Teach Peace to Children*, by Anne Meyer Byler (Herald Press, 2010; download)
- *Love in a Time of Hate: The Story of Magda and André Trocmé and the Village That Said No to the Nazis*, by Hanna Schott, translated by John D. Roth (Herald Press, 2017)
- *Love Undocumented: Risking Trust in a Fearful World*, by Sarah Quezada (Herald Press, 2018)
- *Plant a Seed of Peace*, by Rebecca Seiling (Herald Press, 2007)
- *Plantation Jesus: Race, Faith, and a New Way Forward*, by Skot Welch and Rick Wilson (Herald Press, 2018)
- *Sensing Peace*, by Suzana E. Yoder (Herald Press, 2010)
- *Shalom Sistas: Living Wholeheartedly in a Brokenhearted World*, by Osheta Moore (Herald Press, 2017)
- *Trouble I've Seen: Changing the Way the Church Views Racism*, by Drew G. I. Hart (Herald Press, 2016)

4 FIRST SHALL BE LAST: Winning the "Jesus Way"

Mark 10:31-45

We have lots of races in our family. We race when we're out walking. We race around the dining room table. We even race to the bathroom. We often let the kids win, and when they do, they often congratulate us by saying, "Good job! You won the Jesus way!" As Jesus says in Mark 10:31, "Many who are first will be last, and the last will be first."

I (Peter) trained for four years to break the high school triple jump record, which had stood for 15 years. I came in early to lift weights and ran sprints on the track in the off-season. I battled through muscle and back injuries. Finally, my senior year, I broke the record by about an inch. Two weeks later, a freshman bested my record at a freshman-sophomore meet, and I never got it back.

> **What does it mean, right here and right now, to be in the world but not of it?**

Was all that time and energy wasted? Was it wisely spent? Did I train diligently because I loved track and field, or because I wanted to win the record?

In this session and the next two sessions, we will look at three of the many challenges of upside-down parenting in the midst of prevalent cultural narratives: competition, consumption, and engaging culture. There aren't clear answers with any of these, but we will consider how the life and teachings of Jesus equip us to discern wisely and teach our children well. What does it mean, right here and right now, to be in the world but not of it?

What does competition connected to God's story look like?

Part of the scandal of the gospel is the fact that Jesus actually "lost." He could have "won" the way everyone (including his disciples) expected him to—through a tremendous show of military might. But he simply refused to beat the powers at their own game. Victory instead came through death on a cross. Losing was, oddly enough, how Jesus "won" (Mark 10:32-34). In fact, by losing, Jesus exposed the bankruptcy of the whole system of "keeping score."

Both of us have enjoyed church-related competition: from church softball or basketball teams to parachurch organizations like the Fellowship of Christian Athletes. And as our children grow, sports give them structures in which to discover the wonders of their bodies and the joy of learning something new.

Some of the games we play with our kids, like our household races, are competitive, and we use those as opportunities to practice being humble in success and gracious in defeat. The losers congratulate the winners, and the winners find a way to compliment and encourage the losers. After all, in real life, we do experience both triumph and defeat.

> Some of our favorite games involve collaboration. We all win together, or we all lose together.

Some of our favorite games involve collaboration. We all win together, or we all lose together. In these games, we don't play against each other, but against the game itself, working together toward a common goal. This, too, reflects real life, in which we can accomplish more together.

What are our children learning as they play competitive games?

Sports in North America are a $73.5 billion industry. In fact, modern economies are built on competition. Jesus said that "the last will be first, and the first will be last," but we rarely see that truth enacted in athletics.

Competition appears to be deeply ingrained within the human psyche. Even Jesus' disciples, just after hearing him say that the first shall be last and the last shall be first, were still vying for the coveted prize of sitting next to Jesus.

James and John came to Jesus and asked to be seated next to him when his kingdom came in full. Theirs was a misguided request, as they still saw success and greatness as it is defined by the world: power over others, and glory through might and conquest. But Jesus' kingdom proclaims that great leadership is achieved through service rather than tyranny, and victory through self-giving love rather than violent conquest. Jesus proclaimed an upside-down kingdom so that his followers might view true success and true greatness through the eyes of God. Jesus sought to transform the disciples into people passionate about the things for which God is passionate.

The stories of sports shape our passions to the extent that many fans can quote box scores, records, and statistics with greater ease than many pastors can quote Scripture. The crowds filling enormous stadiums proclaim a story of "community" at a grander scale than churches can muster. More than 50 percent of all U.S. high school students participate in athletics, and the number of hours dedicated to competition far outstrips the amount of time spent in training for discipleship. Parents frantically rush their children to practices and games, often missing worship and other church functions.

We profess the upside-down way of Jesus. But competition, especially in professional athletics, has a way of transforming and capturing our passions. Are our hearts being trained in the upside-down way of Jesus—of self-giving love and humility—or in fallen ways of domination and success?

This is not to say that competition has no redeeming qualities. Athletics offer an opportunity to delight in the wonders of our bodies and learn to work together. While we recognize these redeeming qualities, it's also important to be aware that these seemingly innocuous stories of sports and competition might be transforming us in ways we may not even realize.

As we compete, how can we remember how greatness is viewed in the kingdom of God? How can we embrace a competitive ethos oriented to winning "the Jesus way"?

Talk about it

- ▶ Immerse yourself in the story of Mark 10:31-45. Read through this passage two or three times, preferably out loud. Notice the words or phrases that stand out to you. What strikes you? What questions does this passage raise? How might it speak to parts of our lives affected by sports and competitions?

- ▶ From your youth, what are your best memories of winning? What are your worst memories of losing? To what extent do those wins or losses matter today?

- ▶ In your own experience with competition, what has been the most valuable aspect? How do you continue to pursue that value today?

- ▶ What is your current experience with competition? Against whom do you compete? What does it mean to "win" or "lose"? Who are your adversaries?

- ▶ What are some cooperative games you enjoy? Do your children prefer that kind or the competitive kind? Why?

- What do you make of the values generally ascribed to sports and competition: dedication, hard work, sacrifice, success, and teamwork? How do these compare with the traditional Christian virtues (as listed in the Sermon on the Mount, the fruits of the Spirit, and so on)? How can competition help or hinder our learning of the virtues of greatest importance?

- Where do you draw the line with sports for your children? How do you rank the importance of sports among your children's other activities?

- How do you balance training your children to strive for excellence and reminding them that the last shall be first?

- How do you feel when children's sports interfere with worship, church or family gatherings, or family time?

Suggestions for further reading

- *Good Game: Christianity and the Culture of Sports*, by Shirl J. Hoffman (Baylor University Press, 2010)
- *Hurt 2.0: Inside the World of Today's Teenagers*, by Chap Clark (Baker Academic, 2011)
- *Overplayed: A Parent's Guide to Sanity in the World of Youth Sports*, by David King and Margot Starbuck (Herald Press, 2016)
- *Playing with God: Religion and Modern Sport*, by William J. Baker (Harvard University Press, 2007)

5 WHERE OUR HEART IS: How We Consume in the Upside-Down Kingdom

Luke 12:16-34

Media and advertising can convince us that our worth and success are ultimately defined by what we own. These stories would have us believe that it isn't enough to simply own things that function well; rather, we need the latest and greatest that money can buy. (Whether we can actually afford them is a different question.) These stories would have us believe that our success is tied to what we own and that we work hard to earn money so that we can buy things—without ever considering how these purchases affect others or creation.

As people who believe and proclaim God's story, we know that our worth is not tied to what we own. Yet it is so easy to fall into the pattern of believing the stories that try to convince us otherwise. Although we are not defined by our possessions, what we purchase and how we consume *does* make a difference— not only to ourselves but to creation itself, as well as to other people who may have manufactured or sold us each product. Our purchases and monetary habits reveal where our hearts truly lie.

When our daughter turned one year old, we decided to mark the occasion by asking family and friends to purchase items for Mennonite Central Committee's infant care kits. These kits are sent around the world and given to families displaced by war or disaster. With items like onesies and socks and blankets, the kits support parents who lack the supplies they need to care for a baby.

> We pray that the children and parents who receive these items will know that they are loved.

We still offer this option in lieu of gifts and assemble infant kits around our children's birthdays. Although these items aren't always as exciting to unwrap as some of the other gifts our children receive, they still enjoy shopping to purchase these items, assembling the kits, and delivering them to our local MCC office. These excursions provide us with a wonderful opportunity to explain why this is important. We often wonder together about the places these kits will be sent and who will receive them. And we pray that the children and parents who receive these items will know that they are loved.

5. **WHERE OUR HEART IS:** HOW WE CONSUME IN THE UPSIDE-DOWN KINGDOM

How and why we use our time, talents, and treasures matter.
Where we make our purchases, why we make our purchases, and for whom we make our purchases have lasting influence. We hope that this tradition of assembling infant care kits on behalf of others, rather than simply cluttering our own house

> This practice reminds us and them that our choices matter; it reminds us and them of Jesus' story, which defines us and our consumer choices.

with items we don't need, will affect our children's consumer habits in the future. This practice reminds us and them that our choices matter; it reminds us and them of Jesus' story, which defines us and our consumer choices.

Jesus told a parable about a rich man
whose crops produced so abundantly that he needed to tear down his old barns to build bigger ones in order to contain his overflowing harvest (see Luke 12:16-21). He was overjoyed and sought to indulge in all the pleasures and luxuries that life could offer. He believed it was his well-stocked barns and vast wealth that brought him the merriment he desired and deserved.

Jesus doesn't say whether this man intentionally refused to share his abundance with his poorer neighbors or was just so caught up in his self-indulgence and revelry that he simply couldn't see the poverty and hunger around him. Regardless, he chose to keep his affluence to himself. Therefore, his life was demanded of him—either by God or by his hungry neighbors driven to extremes simply to sate their empty bellies or answer the cries of their hungry children. In the end, "What does it profit them if they gain the whole world, but lose or forfeit themselves?" (Luke 9:25).

Jesus continues by telling his listeners not to worry about their possessions, what they would eat, or what they would wear. It's easy to wonder whether Jesus was being realistic, especially given the myriad things to worry about: work, finances, responsibilities, church, not to mention parenting itself. It's hard to comprehend what a worry-free life might look like.

Does not worrying mean simply turning a blind eye to the ways that our Western consuming habits are depleting and destroying creation? Or that we don't need to worry about our hungry neighbors? What does God's promise of provision mean to those who really do worry about whether they'll be able to feed their children?

> Maybe our anxieties can prompt us to use what we have for the sake of others.

We know that God cares for creation, from the lowliest sparrow to each precious human being. We know that God desires that everyone's needs be met. Because we live in a fallen world, this does not always happen. Yet God is still present, even in our deepest moments of anxiety and fear, reminding us not to be afraid. The stories of this world will not have the final say.

Our worries may not add a single hour to our lives. Perhaps, instead of overwhelming us, they can move us to act in ways that are in keeping with God's story. Maybe our anxieties can prompt us to use what we have for the sake of others, giving generously of our time, talents, and treasures for the sake of the kingdom.

In response to the worries of daily life, we can follow the lead of our children—who, having more recently come from God, remember a wisdom that we as adults forget. Children often remind us to take more time to simply consider the birds of the air, the lilies of the field, and the One who created and cares for each of them.

Talk about it

- Immerse yourself in the story of Luke 12:16-34. Read through this passage two or three times, preferably out loud. Notice the words or phrases that stand out to you. What strikes you? What questions does it raise? How do you experience God speaking to you through these parables and teachings?

- What causes you anxiety? What aspect of life do you find yourself worrying about the most? How has parenting contributed to your anxiety? How have your children helped to relieve this anxiety?

- If you were to ask your children where they think your heart truly lies, what might they answer? On the basis of where you most frequently spend your time, talents, and treasures, what might they say that you, as their parents, treasure?

- What are ways that you model generosity for the sake of your children, other people, and creation? What are some of your practices of purchasing and consuming that are in keeping with God's story? What are some new financial practices or habits of consuming that you would like to implement?

Suggestions for further reading

- *Everyday Justice: The Global Impact of Our Daily Choices*, by Julie Clawson (InterVarsity Press, 2009)
- *Extending the Table*, revised edition, by Joetta Handrich Schlabach (Herald Press, 2014)
- *Four Gifts: Seeking Self-Care for Heart, Soul, Mind, and Strength*, by April Yamasaki (Herald Press, 2018)
- *Living More with Less*, 30th anniversary edition, by Doris Janzen Longacre, edited by Valerie Weaver-Zercher (Herald Press, 2010)
- *More-with-Less*, A World Community Cookbook, 40th anniversary edition, by Doris Janzen Longacre, with Rachel Marie Stone (Herald Press, 2016)
- *Sacred Pauses: Spiritual Practices for Personal Renewal*, by April Yamasaki (Herald Press, 2013)
- *Simply in Season*, 10th anniversary edition, by Mary Beth Lind and Cathleen Hockman-Wert (Herald Press, 2016)
- *Whatever Happened to Dinner? Recipes and Reflections for Family Mealtime*, by Melodie M. Davis (Herald Press, 2010)

6 IN THE WORLD BUT NOT OF IT: [Engaging Culture with Our Kids]

John 17

There are stories all around us that transform us (and our children) in ways that we may or may not even be aware of. We have chosen to embody God's story, yet we still live within the world. Because we live in the world, we are also shaped by the narratives of culture, both the larger culture and the intersecting groups in which we find ourselves a part of—cultures informed by our ethnicity, race, location, gender, income level, social circles, and so on.

Culture isn't necessarily a negative thing. There may be many parts of our culture that we embrace and which seem in keeping with who God has called us to be.

Yet it is important to prayerfully discern how stories, practices, and behaviors from culture are shaping us. How are these messages forming our perceptions of God, ourselves, other people, and the world around us? How are they teaching us to engage with others? How are they transforming where it is our heart truly lies?

> It's important to be aware of the ways that cultural narratives are forming us.

As people shaped by God's story, it's important to be aware of the ways that cultural narratives are forming us and to equip our children with tools to engage culture in a meaningful way.

We enjoy playing games, reading, and watching movies with our children. For one thing, they're still at the age when they want to be with us. (We've heard that doesn't necessarily last!) For another, even though there are times when it's tempting to play a movie for the kids and get some of our work done, we've made it a priority to do things with them so we can help them process what they're experiencing. In addition, we have intentionally tried to expose ourselves and our children to stories in which the characters look different from us or come from different cultures or countries.

Sometimes we see something in a film or a book and point out, "That was a kind choice! Look at how that helps everyone!" Other times we say, "That was a mean choice. I wonder what would have happened if they had chosen to respond differently," or "This is the way some people behave, but as people who follow Jesus, we choose a different way."

The older they get, the more they are exposed to different stories, ideas, and practices—some of which are in keeping with God's story and some of which are not. We won't always be with them to point out certain assumptions or help them consider certain situations. Yet we hope we're providing them with tools to process the stories around them, to recognize what is life giving and what is not, to be in the world but not of the world.

Before Jesus' crucifixion in the gospel of John, Jesus

spends a great deal of time teaching and equipping his disciples so that they will remember what it means to be his followers. As he finishes his exhortations to his disciples, he prays for them, that they might continue to follow his ways even after he is no longer with them (see John 17). He has done what he could with the time he was given to equip them to engage with the world in meaningful ways. Jesus knows that God's ways are not like the ways of the kingdoms of this world, and he knows that he and his disciples are not "of this world" and therefore shouldn't give ultimate allegiance to the narratives of this world.

> [**His disciples are not to withdraw and separate themselves; instead, they are to remain where they are.**]

But Jesus also doesn't want his disciples to be entirely removed from the world. His disciples are not to withdraw and separate themselves; instead, they are to remain where they are: engaging the world, pointing to the places where God's movement is already present, and witnessing to God's story in the places where it is desperately needed. Jesus has equipped his followers to remain in the world without being ultimately transformed by it.

As parents, we can frequently remind our children that we belong to God and that it is God's story that informs our daily choices. We can look for those teachable moments to point out the times when we see God's story shining through a book or a movie or a

> It's our job as parents to give our children tools to help them process and think critically about the practices they're seeing in the media and among their peers.

news story or a friend's choice, as well as those times when we see the world making choices contrary to God's ways. It's our job as parents to give our children tools to help them process and think critically about the practices they're seeing in the media and among their peers. We hope to lay a firm foundation to remind them of God's story. We hope to hone their vision to notice the times when the world's stories point to or contradict God's story.

Just as Jesus prayed for his disciples, we can pray for our children. We can pray that when it matters, they will remember what we have taught them (even when it doesn't always seem that they are listening!). We pray, trusting that God's Spirit will teach and remind our children of the story that really matters: the Jesus story we're called to embody and proclaim.

We pray that we and our children can meaningfully engage the world, bringing light in the midst of darkness and hope to places of hopelessness so that God may be glorified.

6. **In the World but Not of It:** Engaging Culture with Our Kids

Talk about it

▶ Immerse yourself in the story of John 17. Read through this prayer two or three times, preferably out loud. Notice the words or phrases that stand out to you. What strikes you? What questions does this passage raise? How is this prayer speaking to ways we might engage the culture?

▶ Immerse yourself in the story of Acts 17:22-34. Read through this story two or three times, out loud if possible. Notice the words or phrases that stand out to you. What strikes you? What questions does this passage raise? How is this story speaking to ways we might engage the culture?

▶ What cultures would you consider yourself to be a part of or shaped by? What feels life giving in regard to these cultures? What about these cultures perhaps bears more thoughtful consideration?

▶ What do you think it means to be *in* the world but not *of* the world?

▶ Think about the stories that we are being exposed to on a daily basis. Think about movies or books you read, sporting events you engage in or watch, school experiences, social media, technology, advertisements, and so on. What messages do we receive from our culture that are in keeping with the good news of God's story?

▶ What messages do we receive from our culture that run counter to the good news of God's story?

▶ How can we help equip our children to critically engage with cultural narratives? What conversations can we have to help them understand what is and is not in keeping with God's story?

Suggestions for further reading

- *Desiring the Kingdom: Worship, Worldview, and Cultural Formation*, by James K. A. Smith (Baker Academic, 2009)
- *Jesus for President: Politics for Ordinary Radicals*, by Shane Claiborne and Chris Haw (Zondervan, 2008)
- *Parent Trek: Nurturing Creativity and Care in Our Children*, by Jeanne Zimmerly Jantzi; commissioned by Mennonite Central Committee (Herald Press, 2001)
- *The Upside-Down Kingdom*, anniversary edition, by Donald B. Kraybill (Herald Press, 2018)

About the Writers

Katherine and Peter Goerzen have been married for 11 years and have a six-year-old daughter and a four-year-old son. They live in North Newton, Kansas. Katherine and Peter are both graduates of Anabaptist Mennonite Biblical Seminary and are ordained ministers in Mennonite Church USA. They served together as copastors for five years and continue to enjoy engaging each other in theological discussions. Currently, Katherine is serving as associate pastor at Tabor Mennonite Church. Her duties focus on worship planning and youth ministry (which, to her, is an ideal job description). Peter is currently serving at Bethel College as campus pastor and instructor of Bible and religion. Katherine and Peter also enjoy parenting, reading, and watching murder mysteries together.

Discover all the books in the UPSIDE DOWN LIVING series

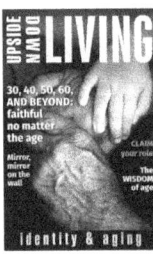

Identity and Aging
We get older every day, and as we age our lives change. In moving from youth to young adulthood, from middle-aged to retiree, we discover that life marches on even as our situations and identities continue to change. This study explores how we can age faithfully and gracefully, embracing ourselves through each phase of life.

Money
Every day we face decisions that impact our wallets—and these decisions say a lot about our priorities. The way we use money can communicate power and strength, charity and selflessness. How does your use of money reflect or expand your faith? This study takes an honest look at financial choices and how we can view them through a lens of faith.

Parenting
Raising kids is hard enough. But raising kids to heed Jesus' upside-down call away from status and power and toward service and sharing? It can seem almost impossible. So how can parents model countercultural choices? What habits can help families joyfully follow Christ instead of the latest trend? Gather with your faith community to search the Scriptures and discuss how to raise faithful kids in the twenty-first century.

Prayer
Prayer can easily become an afterthought, a hasty sentence, a laundry list of all the things we want. But what if prayer is a time to find out what God wants for us—and for our world? What does it mean to pray that the kingdom would come here and now as it is in heaven? Explore these questions in this study, and learn prayer practices that nurture intimacy with God and sensitivity to God's dream for the world.

Sabbath
People are busy. Between work, family, church, and other obligations, it's difficult to slow down and take a break. Yet taking time to pause for a Sabbath rest is what can refresh our souls the most—bringing renewed focus and clarity to our relationship with God and with those close to us. This study looks at Sabbath and how it is an effective way to recharge our lives and reconnect with what matters most.

Sharing Faith Stories
Every person of faith has a story. At times our lives are interesting and compelling, mundane and routine. Yet taken together these individual moments create a mosaic that can be shared with others. This study will empower you to discover how to communicate your own story with others as an effective way of sharing your faith.

Technology
Technology keeps us connected around the clock. But what happens when the technology tools created to help us control us instead? How do we determine our technology needs against our wants? Explore these questions and more in this study, and discover a way to navigate technology's pitfalls.

Violence
We see it on the news every day. We see it in our neighborhoods. Violence is almost a fact of life, impacting the world, our communities, our friends, our families. How do people of faith respond? How do we get involved in speaking up for peace, in addressing the violence in our communities? This study explores responses to these difficult questions and situations.

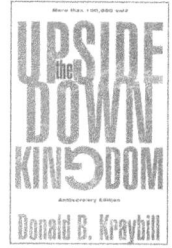

The Upside-Down Kingdom *Anniversary Edition*
Donald B. Kraybill

In the anniversary edition of the classic book *The Upside-Down Kingdom*, author Donald B. Kraybill calls readers to imagine and embody the reign of God on earth as it is in heaven. Since its publication in 1978, *The Upside-Down Kingdom* won the National Religious Book Award and has become the most trusted resource on radical Christian discipleship. What does it mean to follow the Christ who traded victory and power for hanging out with the poor and forgiving his enemies? How did a man in first-century Palestine threaten the established order, and what does that mean for us today? What would happen if Christians replaced force with suffering, violence with love, and nationalism with allegiance to Jesus?

Jesus turned expectations upside-down. The kingdom of God is still full of surprises. Are you ready?

www.HeraldPress.com
800-245-7894

www.ingramcontent.com/pod-product-compliance
Lightning Source LLC
Chambersburg PA
CBHW031451070426
42452CB00038B/834